True Tales of the Everglades

By Stuart McIver

Florida Flair Books

Miami, Florida

Stuart McIver has obtained the bulk of the information contained in this book from a combination of interviews with
oldtimers, and exhaustive research through the files and source
material of eight South Florida historical societies. Regional
histories, and old newspaper and magazine articles have
yielded additional information.

Contents

PART ONE

The Everglades

The Death of an Audubon Warden

Hidden away, deep in the Cape Sable mangroves, the tiny island called Cuthbert Rookery gave sanctuary to flocks of battered wading birds, fighting a losing battle against the rifle and the shotgun of the plume hunter. All that protected them were the remoteness of the islet and the tough resourcefulness of an Audubon warden named Guy Bradley.

The warden knew the ways of the birds—and the plume hunters. And why not? After all, he had been a plumer himself at a time when killing plume birds had been legal. As a boy growing up near Palm Beach, he had shot birds and picked up spending money by selling their plumes to agents of the big hat manufacturers in faraway New York City. Women's hats decorated with bird feathers had become so popular by the turn of the century that choice egret plumes sold for $32 an ounce, more than the price of gold at the time.

High prices led to slaughter, whole rookeries were "shot out" by greedy hunters. It was a practice that sickened many outdoorsmen, including Bradley. In 1901 the State of Florida outlawed plume hunting. A year later Guy was hired by the National Association of Audubon Societies to guard the birds at the tip of Florida. His was a vast territory that included the Florida Keys, the Everglades, Big Cypress Swamp and the Ten Thousand Islands. The jewel in the vast wilderness he patrolled was the Cuthbert, the last great, and to American ornithologists, the most precious rookery in the country.

Guy lived in Flamingo, a wild frontier settlement with less than a hundred residents, a mixture of fugitives, misfits and renegades. Bradley owned a house and a quarter of a mile of land fronting on Florida Bay. It was home to Guy, his wife Fronie and their two small sons.

In 1897 Bradley's father had moved his family to Flamingo, where he represented the Model Land Company. Henry M. Flagler created the company to develop the vast land holdings the State gave him in return for building his railroad along the southeast coast.

Bradley traveled back and forth across his territory, first in a small sailboat and later in a primitive power boat. He posted warnings and visited with hunters, hermits, farmers and fishermen, educating them about the new law that made the killing of plume birds illegal. Under his care the Cuthbert bird population began to grow. Colonies of egrets, herons, spoonbills and ibises had found a haven again.

Occasionally he had to arrest plume hunters, always a tricky task, since they usually had guns in their hands when challenged.

Twice he had to arrest a man named Captain Walter Smith and his 16-year-old son, Tom. After Tom's second arrest, Smith's fury exploded:

"You ever arrest one of my boys again, I'll kill you."

The captain, a Civil War veteran who had served as a sharp-shooter in the Confederate Army, presented a particularly sticky problem. Before they moved to Flamingo, the Smiths and the Bradleys had been neighbors in Lantana. Smith's wife and Guy's mother were close friends, drawn together by a mutual love of music. Tragically, the families, torn by the arrests and local politics, grew apart.

On the morning of July 8, 1905 the waters of Florida Bay lay flat and still, sky blending into water without horizon. Suddenly, the sound of gunfire shattered the early morning quiet. Guy stepped out the front door, squinted his eyes and looked out across the bay. Just beyond the island in front of his home lay Oyster Keys, two small islands about two miles away. A schooner was anchored near the keys. Guy recognized it as Captain Smith's *Cleveland.*

Bradley knew what he had to do, and he knew he had to do it alone, both his deputy wardens were away. Guy got his pistol, walked down to the water and launched his small sailboat . . . there was no wind, he would have to row.

His wife Fronie was there at the water to say good-bye. Tension and fear were in the air as he rowed out into the bay. She went back into the house to escape the blazing sun, it was nine a.m.

Guy Bradley never returned. Before the morning was over he would become the first Audubon warden to die in the line of duty.

Guy Bradley, ca. 1902

A grim-faced Captain Smith sailed back to his home and told his family: "We've got to load up and get out of here. I'm going to Key West and give myself up. I've killed Guy Bradley."

In Key West, Smith pleaded self defense. His son Tom, with his younger brother, Danny, had gone ashore, he said, at Oyster Keys where they shot egrets and cormorants. As Bradley approached his boat, Smith fired his rifle as a signal to his boys. They brought the birds aboard *Cleveland* in plain sight of Bradley.

"I want your son Tom," Guy called to Smith.

"Well, if you want him, you have got to have a warrant."

Bradley denied a warrant was necessary.

"Well, if you want him you have to come aboard this boat and take him." Smith picked up his Winchester .38 rifle.

"Put down that rifle and I will come aboard."

Bradley drew his pistol, Smith claimed, and fired up at him, missing him and striking the main mast. The old sharpshooter then aimed his Winchester down at Bradley and fired with deadly accuracy.

Smith had strong political connections in the county seat. Even though he had killed an officer of the law in the act of making an arrest, grand jurors in December voted not to indict the captain.

Justice was not served, but Bradley's death was not in vain nor was it forgotten. Revulsion at the killing of an Audubon warden led to legislation in New York State and in Washington, D.C. that would within a decade effectively end the plume trade in America.

Guy Bradley was buried at the tip of Cape Sable. A plaque in his honor was lovingly placed above the grave by the Florida Audubon Society.

In 1960 Hurricane Donna struck South Florida. Guy's grave was washed away and the Cuthbert Rookery, which he had worked so hard to preserve, was devastated.

With time the rookery began to recover both its vegetation and its birds. A handsome monument to Bradley has been erected at the Visitors Center in Flamingo, a reminder that a brave man gave his life here protecting the plume birds.

The Women Who Saved Paradise Key

In 1893, the dean of the University of Florida College of Agriculture and the director of the New York Botanical Garden sloshed their way through the waters of the Everglades till they reached a mile-wide hammock.

The two men had heard about the hammock, which enjoyed a modest fame for its magnificent stand of royal palms growing wild. Their photographs of lush tropical vegetation prompted the first calls to preserve the area.

Over a half-century later, Paradise Key would become an important step in the establishment of Everglades National Park. But it took a group of determined women to make it happen.

Most of the land near Paradise Key belonged to the Model Land Company, the real estate arm of the vast Florida empire created by railroad king Henry Flagler.

Amid rumors that buyers were interested in the land for development as citrus groves, J.E. Ingraham, a top Flagler executive, met with Mary Barr Munroe, chairman of the Florida Federation of Women's Clubs, to discuss the future of the hammock.

Mrs. Munroe, wife of the novelist Kirk Munroe, was a fiery activist. To protest women wearing egret plumes on their hats, she was known to walk up to total strangers and suddenly and violently yank the hats from their heads. The results were spectacular, especially when the hats were pinned to the women's hair.

If she wasn't afraid to attack the heads of fashionable women, Mary Munroe certainly wasn't going to be shy about telling Ingraham what she wanted: the donation of Paradise Key to the Federation to preserve a park.

Ingraham agreed with her, and managed to persuade Mary Lily Kenan Flagler, Henry's widow, to give nearly a thousand acres to the federation. The state matched it with an additional thousand acres.

On November 22, 1916, Ingraham Highway, the road the Model Land Company had built to the hammock, carried 150 automobiles filled with 750 people to the dedication of Royal Palm State Park.

The first caretaker, Charles A. Mosier, lived with his fam-

Charles Torrey Simpson, left, and Charles Mosier at Royal Palm Lodge on Paradise Key, ca. 1920. (*Historical Association of Southern Florida*)

ily in a tent for three years until the completion of a lodge to house and feed visitors to the park.

Despite fire and the hurricane of 1926, the Women's Club kept the park going until it was taken over by the federal government in 1947.

Flamingo Was the End of the World

When the settlers at the tip of Cape Sable established a post office in 1893, they were told they had to give their settlement a name.

They considered End of the World. Instead, they picked a romantic, exotic name for their own personal hell-hole. They called it Flamingo, shortened on occasion to Mingo and lengthened on others to Fillymingo.

In the 1890s, flocks of the spectacular tropical birds were commonly seen in the Cape Sable area, although South Florida was at the end of the bird's range, so the name made sense. So did End of the World, since the Cape at that time was an isolated society populated mostly by people who were running away from something—the law, civilization, or maybe their wives.

When they reached the Cape, they knew they had arrived at the end of mainland Florida. There was nowhere else to go.

"Uncle" Steve Roberts came to Flamingo in 1901. He was born in Micanopy and his father is said to have laid out the town of Gainesville. Some say Roberts came south for his wife's health, some say for his own, since there were reports linking him with cattle rustling.

Whatever the reason, Uncle Steve stayed on and became Flamingo's power structure. With him he brought his five sons and three daughters, a population explosion in its own right, in a town of only a half-dozen families.

People at the Cape made their living fishing, raising sugar cane, making moonshine and smuggling. Uncle Steve was active in a number of these frontier pursuits. Though he was reported to be a plume hunter, two of his sons were Audubon wardens trying to stamp out the illegal trade.

One of the settlers' worst enemies were mosquitos. Stories abound that they had been known to kill cows and mules left out for the night.

Every house was equipped with smudge pots and a palmetto fan. When you entered a Cape Sable shack, you brushed yourself off with the palmetto in a room called a "loser." It was where you were supposed to lose your mosquitos.

Most of the houses were built on stilts to guard against hurricanes or high tides from Florida Bay. Uncle Steve's home

The Roberts Hotel in Flamingo, ca. 1920. (*Historical Association of Southern Florida*)

became the Roberts Hotel in 1915. His two-story house had four bedrooms upstairs for regular or transient boarders. Extra mattresses on the floor took care of overflow guests. The old hotel was destroyed by a hurricane in 1926.

Making syrup and moonshine whiskey from sugar cane was a major industry at Flamingo. In 1908, the cane was besieged by a horde of rats. Uncle Steve's son, Gene, came up with an idea to save the town.

"Men," he told a gathering, "we've done everything we could think of to get rid of the rats, but it ain't done no good . . . These few cats we got here has done the best they can, but they can't eat but so many rats. So I say we ought to chip in and run down to Key West and buy up a whole bunch of cats and bring 'em here."

Gene took up a collection, then set sail for Key West. A sign reading "Will Pay 10 cents Apiece for Every Cat Delivered to this Dock" brought him a cargo of 400 cats to take back to Cape Sable.

"That 90-mile trip was the worst I ever made," said Gene.

The cats took one look at Flamingo, then disappeared into the wilderness. But they did wipe out the rats.

In 1922, a road was completed linking Flamingo with Homestead. Many hoped the town would blossom. Just the opposite happened. It lost population. People had found a way to get out. Now the town at the end of the world is a resort at the end of Everglades National Park.

Steamboating in the Everglades

The age of the steamboat in Florida lasted roughly 30 years until 1921. They were years which saw the beginnings of development in a wild and beautiful land. The steam age also featured a comical Florida version of the driving of the "golden spike" that connected America's railroads from the Atlantic to the Pacific.

Florida Governor Albert W. Gilchrist was the instigator. Some 50 newspapermen from papers and wire services all over the country were riding with him as the steamboat *Thomas A. Edison* huffed its way up the Caloosahatchee River from Fort Myers to LaBelle. There they switched to the smaller *Queen of the Glades*.

The *Queen* carried the group up to Lake Okeechobee and then on to Ritta, on the south shore of the lake. There they spent the night at a hotel. The next day, April 26, 1912, Governor Gilchrist was going to do a trick with a couple of coconuts that would symbolize what the much ballyhooed trip was all about.

In 1906, the State of Florida had launched a massive program designed to drain the Everglades and thus produce dry, fertile farm land. The project had delivered less than it promised. As a result, papers all over the United States were running stories about the "Florida scandal."

Now after six struggling years, the first canal from the lower east coast to the lake had been completed. The governor wanted a critical press to know that something had finally been accomplished.

That morning the party reboarded the *Queen* and steamed into the North New River Canal. Out came the governor's coconut shells. One contained water from the Gulf of Mexico, the other water from the Atlantic. With ceremonial flourish, Gilchrist mixed the water from the two coconuts. By uniting the waters of the Gulf and the Atlantic, the governor was dramatizing Florida's first cross-state waterway. Now for the first time a boat could sail across Florida from Fort Myers to Fort Lauderdale.

To prove it, the party continued on down the narrow drainage canal through the Everglades, past sawgrass, tree islands and huge flocks of wading birds. When they arrived in

13

Suwanee, most popular of all Everglades steamboats, ca. 1915. (*Fort Lauderdale Historical Society*)

Fort Lauderdale, they were greeted, reports say, by every man, woman and child in the little frontier town. To the governor's political eye, it added up to about 50 voters.

The most popular of all the steamboats serving the east coast port of Fort Lauderdale was the *Suwanee*. For early settlers who could muster a round trip fare of $25, the steamboat carried 32 passengers from Fort Lauderdale through the Everglades and on across to Fort Myers and back.

Eventually silting and water hyacinths ended the golden era when a 70-foot sternwheeler could make its way through the New River Canal. The last passenger steamboat from Lake Okeechobee to Fort Lauderdale was *Passing Thru*, a 42-foot glass cabin boat, used first to haul freight through the Hillsboro Canal, then converted to hauling people on both the Hillsboro and the New River Canals. Ports of call for *Passing*

See the Everglades—A Big Country With a Big Future

STONE'S BOAT LINE
TO THE EVERGLADES

Boat "Passing Thru"

Ft. Lauderdale, Okeelanta, South Bay Torry Island, Chosen, Belle Glade and Hillsboro Canal

Leave Ft. Lauderdale 7:30 a. m., Monday and Thursday
Leave Torry Island 7:30 a. m., Tuesday and Saturday.

Oct. to Dec. 25 1921.

CAPT. LAWRENCE E. WILL, Manager

Last Passenger boat from Lake points to Ft. Lauderdale

Ad for Stone's Boat Line, 1921. (*Sunshine Magazine*)

Thru included Okeelanta, South Bay, Torry Island, Chosen, Belle Glade and Fort Lauderdale.

At the helm of the boat on its last Fort Lauderdale run was skipper Lawrence Will, self-styled "Cracker historian of the Everglades." In his *Okeechobee Boats and Skippers*, he wrote ". . . we kept chugging along and finally tied up in Fort Lauderdale at the foot of Brickell Avenue. It was 3:30 Christmas morning. I toted some of the lady passenger's go-way bags to the hotel, and I reckon that was about the last time I've walked barefooted up the main street of Fort Lauderdale— well, the last time on a Christmas Day at any rate."

The voyage of the *Passing Thru* marked the end of a glorious era that the *Suwanee* had ushered in for South Florida.

Ad for Stone's Boat Line, 1921. (*Sunshine Magazine*)

Thru included Okeelanta, South Bay, Torry Island, Chosen, Belle Glade and Fort Lauderdale.

At the helm of the boat on its last Fort Lauderdale run was skipper Lawrence Will, self-styled "Cracker historian of the Everglades." In his *Okeechobee Boats and Skippers*, he wrote ". . . we kept chugging along and finally tied up in Fort Lauderdale at the foot of Brickell Avenue. It was 3:30 Christmas morning. I toted some of the lady passenger's go-way bags to the hotel, and I reckon that was about the last time I've walked barefooted up the main street of Fort Lauderdale— well, the last time on a Christmas Day at any rate."

The voyage of the *Passing Thru* marked the end of a glorious era that the *Suwanee* had ushered in for South Florida.

Dredging the Everglades

The stout-hearted crew of the dipper-dredge *The Everglades* should have known they were in for trouble when they started work on a holiday, July 4, 1906.

It certainly turned out to be anything but a holiday for the crew of 18, captained by Henry Clay Cassidey, whose handlebar mustache bespoke authority. A second dredge, the *Okeechobee*, started operations on April Fool's Day, 1907. It figured.

Captain Cassidey and his crew faced a difficult task: to dig a canal from the south fork of the New River west through the Everglades and north toward Lake Okeechobee. It was the first cut through the wilderness to fulfill Florida Governor Napoleon Bonaparte Broward's campaign promise to drain the Everglades.

Reed Bryan had been hired to supervise the construction of *The Everglades* and the *Okeechobee*. Working with machinery the state had purchased from a Chicago firm, Bryan set about building the dredges just across the river from where he, his brother Tom, and his father P. N. Bryan, were building the Bryan Hotel, later renamed the New River Inn and now the Discovery Center.

By April, 1906, Bryan had *The Everglades* ready to go. Governor Broward came down from Tallahassee for the christening of the first two dredges. Reed's sister Constance smashed a bottle of champagne across the bow, and the face of South Florida was permanently changed.

Some time later, another dredge was to start south from the big lake, and with a little luck there was always the chance they might make connections and wind up with a 75-mile-long canal connecting Fort Lauderdale with Lake Okeechobee.

But luck does not always come to those in a hurry, and Broward's survey team was in a hurry, often surveying just ahead of the dredges, hammering in stakes for the giant machines to follow.

Mosquitos, snakes and the heat of the summer wore on the dredgers. By the end of 1907 the two dredges, which had been built at Sailboat Bend near present-day Third Avenue on the New River, had managed to dig only four and one-half miles of canal and reclaimed only about 12,000 acres. One of

The Everglades, the first of the dredge boats, Captain Cassidey at left, 1906. (*Fort Lauderdale Historical Society*)

the project's doubters charged that at that rate it would take a century to reclaim a million acres.

Three years after *The Everglades* set out from Fort Lauderdale, another dredge, *Caloosahatchee*, started south from the lake. After about six miles the chief engineer surveyed a curve, instructed the crew to begin work the next day at a certain compass reading, then left for Fort Myers. The next morning the compass acted erratically, perhaps because of a severe electrical storm. At any rate, a six-mile error occurred.

Patching up the problem was difficult. Later, in trying to make connections with the dredge from the south, three men in two canoes set out to find *The Everglades*. The trio had to be rescued by the Fort Lauderdale crew, who found them exhausted, bitten up by mosquitos and weak from lack of food.

Somehow, in April of 1912, the job was completed. But the unruly compass left its legacy—a jog in the canal near the eastern entrance to Alligator Alley.

Broward, who came here often to visit Reed's project, is remembered in a different way. In 1915, when a new county was created out of parts of Dade and Palm Beach counties, it was named after the governor who dug ditches through South Florida, creating fortunes and controversy in the wake of the slow dredges.

Unconquered Seminoles and Miccosukees

Three times the Seminoles and the United States fought, the longest war lasting seven bloody years. Many Indians were killed, many deported to Arkansas. The Seminoles were driven down to the tip of the peninsula and back and forth across the Everglades. A nation of 5000 dwindled down to a remnant of 100.

But that remnant never surrendered, never signed a peace treaty. From these 100 sprang today's Seminole and Miccosukee Tribes. They were the unconquered.

In the 1700s Indians from the Creek Confederation began drifting across the border from the British colonies of Georgia and Alabama into sparsely-settled Spanish Florida. These Indians included Alachuas, Muskogees, Hitchitis and Tallahassees.

At about the same time the Miccosukee began to settle in the Florida Panhandle, some near Lake Miccosukee, close to today's Tallahassee.

The Muskogees had a word for people who moved away to less populous areas. They called them "sim-in-oli," which meant "wild." In time the Indians who had migrated to Florida from southern colonies came to be regarded as one people called "Seminoles."

In the early nineteenth century a new nation, aggressive and energetic, was feeling its oats. Angry at the escape of black slaves cross the border to Indian settlements in Florida, the United States fought the tribes in the Panhandle in the First Seminole War, 1817–1818. The war drove many Indians deeper into Central Florida.

After the United States acquired Florida from Spain, Americans began pouring into the new territory, clamoring for land and for the return of their slaves. When Florida's new owners started deporting Indians to Arkansas, Seminoles and Miccosukees banded together and struck back in December of 1835.

Seven years of warfare followed. Not even 50,000 American troops could bring a force of 1800 Indian warriors to the peace table. The Second Seminole War ended in 1842 without a peace treaty.

A Third Seminole War, 1855–1858, further weakened the

Indians. The number of Indians in Florida dwindled to less than 100. But still there was no peace treaty.

From that proud remnant has grown today's tourist-oriented Indian population. The Seminoles, 1800 strong, live in reservations in Hollywood and in the areas northwest and south of Lake Okeechobee. Some 550 Miccosukees live, mostly in the Everglades, many of them along the Tamiami Trail.

Seminoles and Miccosukees intermarry, share many common cultural heritages and customs, yet remain separate in their governments and tribal organization. Both are now incorporated, the Seminole Tribe in 1957 and the Miccosukee Tribe of Indians of Florida five years later.

They have known hard times. But to this day they remain an independent, unconquered people, proud of their Indian culture and heritage.

Seminole camp deep in the Everglades, ca. 1930. (*Fort Lauderdale Historical Society*)

An Everglades Friendship

They were born the same year, 1886, in the wild frontier of southwest Florida. But they came from different worlds.

Frank Brown was the child of a white family reaching out to the Indians; Josie Billie was the child of a Miccosukee family reaching out to the white man.

Frank's father was a true Anglo, a native of Bristol, England. Starting from a base in Fort Myers, Bill Brown kept moving his trading post deeper and deeper into the Indian hunting grounds.

In 1901 he established his legendary Brown's Boat Landing on the western edge of the Everglades, 30 miles east of what is now Immokalee.

Josie's father was likewise a trailblazer, known both as Little Billy and Billy Conapatchee. He broke tribal law by attending the white man's school in Fort Myers. For this transgression, members of the tribe decreed that he should be put to death. He stayed out of sight for a year, until the killing fever passed.

Josie Billie inherited his father's thirst for learning. As a boy, he spent many hours at the home of his friend, Frank Brown. From one of the women at the Brown household in the Everglades he learned to read and write English.

Frank, in turn, spent weeks at a time with Josie's family, hunting throughout the Big Cypress. He came to know the swamp as no white man had ever known it before. Throughout his lifetime, he was a sought-after hunting guide.

Josie was married three times, and lived for a while on the Big Cypress Reservation. When the Tamiami Trail opened, he established a camp near Ochopee. As a young man, Josie was fond of whiskey, and in 1928 he stabbed an Indian woman to death during a drunken brawl. He was later found blameless by the tribe.

Josie's quest for self-improvement never stopped. He studied first to become a tribal doctor and in 1937 attained the honored position of medicine man and chief of the Miccosukees.

Sometime around 1943, Josie Billie became a Baptist convert. By 1946, he received his first formal schooling, attending the Florida Baptist Institute at the age of 60.

Josie Billie, left, and Frank Brown, ca. 1900. (*Florida Photographic Archives*)

After his conversion, he became a teetotaler.

Both Josie and Frank, born in the days when Florida was a vast wilderness, survived into the age of color television, condominiums and space travel. Both died in their 80s.

They remained friends to the end.

Tamiami Trail Blazers

In 1915, J. F. Jaudon, Dade County tax assessor and real estate developer, was promoting a unique and daring venture—a highway from Miami to Fort Myers and then on up to Tampa. A man from Tampa suggested it be called the Tamiami Trail.

From opposite sides of South Florida, Dade and Lee County authorities set about building the Trail in their areas, hoping to connect at some future date. Eight years later that date was still way off and the project was badly bogged down, with a 40-mile gap of Everglades and cypress swamp separating the completed parts.

A group of Fort Myers civic and business leaders decided that a dramatic gesture was needed to revive interest in the Trail. They dubbed themselves the Trail Blazers, and their goal was somehow to make it across the gap via automobile, thereby proving that crossing the Everglades by car was possible.

On April 4, 1923, the Trail Blazers, 25 in all, including two Indian guides, set out from Fort Myers. The caravan consisted of eight Fords, a commissary truck and a 3,200-pound Elcar,

Building the Tamiami Trail across the Everglades, ca. 1925. (*Historical Association of Southern Florida*)

entered in the event by a car dealer to prove the vehicle's stamina. The Elcar did fine on the parts of the Trail already completed but it lasted only about 100 yards into the really rough going. It had to be tugged the rest of the way by two tractors.

The trip, planned to take three days, took three weeks. Planes went out to search for the Blazers and failed to spot them. Wild stories circulated. The group was lost in quicksand. They had been captured and tortured by Indians. One story claimed they had taken several women with them and were simply in no hurry to get out.

The truth was a good deal less glamorous. The cars kept sinking into the muck, wheels were broken, an engine burned out. The men had to build makeshift bridges and cut down saplings to lay out a "corduroy" road of wood.

Finally, mosquito-bitten, sawgrass-slashed, famished and weary, the Trail Blazers reached Dade County.

Did their trail blazing speed up completion of the first road across the Everglades? Possibly. At any rate, the Tamiami Trail was finally opened to the public in April, 1928—just five years after the Trail Blazers ended their adventure.

A Miccosukee's View of the Trail

The Tamiami Trail cuts through the heart of the Everglades, it also cuts through the very lives of the Miccosukee Indians.

"This road is like that thing the Russians built, you know, the Berlin Wall," said Homer Osceola, who counts himself among those known as "traditional" Miccosukees. He has spent most of his life in a small Everglades hammock area some 25 miles west of Miami.

As a little boy, he lived in the camp of his father, William McKinley Osceola, an Indian of note, named for the American president assassinated in 1901.

In 1926 huge dredges appeared at the camp. Homer watched as monster machines began scooping up land out of hammocks and sawgrass prairie. Then tractors and rollers packed down the piles of Everglades muck and oolite rock into a roadbed that would become the Tamiami Trail.

As the heavy equipment moved west, it left behind not only a roadbed but also a deep canal. A "borrow" canal, the white man called it, since land was borrowed to build the road.

Many Indians who had eked out a meager living farming or selling pelts, hides or bird plumes to Miami trading posts now earned money by working on the huge construction project. They never realized how much it was destined to reshape their way of life.

In 1928 the Trail was completed. Fancy, noisy automobiles roared past the camps, bringing strangers into the wilderness the Indians had known as their own.

But that was not all that was changed. The roadbed now functioned as a wall and the canal lowered the water level near the old camps. Canoe trails they had used for years vanished. Now everything was different.

Even William McKinley Osceola was different. He bought a car and learned to use it. During the trapping season he made several hundred dollars a month by driving other Indians and their supplies to choice hunting spots along the Trail, then buying the pelts they took for resale to the white jobber in Miami.

From time to time the William McKinley Osceola family, including Homer, lived at Musa Isle Seminole Indian Village,

Cultures meet in the Everglades as Tamiami Trail is cut through the land of the Miccosukees, ca. 1925. (*Photo by Claude Matlack, Historical Association of Southern Florida*)

a Miami amusement park. The attraction showed the tourists the colorful clothing of the Indians, their thatched chickees and their skill in alligator wrestling.

The Miccosukees tended to live at Musa Isle for short periods of time, then return to their more traditional lives in the Glades. More and more often they brought back with them the ways of the white man. Along the Trail they started setting up small complexes where they could sell handicrafts, offer a tour of an authentic Indian village, wrestle alligators, and after World War II take the tourists on airboat rides.

On land just across the Trail from the camp of his father, Homer Osceola tries hard to preserve the traditional ways of the Miccosukee. But like most people he faces the need to make a living. He runs a small attraction, Homer Osceola's Village, where tourists can buy beadwork, jackets, skirts, dresses, soft drinks, and airboat rides.

Just south of the Berlin Wall.

The First Airboat

Once Everglades frog hunters worked at night in the cold and wet, searching across the vast Everglades for the small animal. Now it is illegal to remove or destroy plants and animals from the area of the Everglades National Park.

Johnny Lamb was averaging 75 pounds of frog legs a night, but it was a tough way to earn a living during the Depression. Getting around the Everglades was the problem. The area was too big and wet for walking, and too shallow for power boats.

Over a midnight cup of coffee Lamb and his buddy Russell Howard were grumbling about their problems. Poling a flat-bottom boat was hard going. Using an outboard motor was even worse, because weeds and muck clogged the propellers and the cooling systems.

"How about a wind machine on the stern, not in the water?" mused Howard. If a propeller worked for an airplane, he explained, why not for a shallow-draft boat?

The two men decided to give it a try by using a 12-foot, flat-bottom boat, a 75-horsepower engine, a second-hand aircraft propeller, a ply-wood rudder and a steering wheel.

Their invention became known as an "airboat." Lamb called it "a Rube Goldberg contraption," and they refined it into a vehicle that gave them a big edge over the other frog hunters. But they decided not to go through the red tape and expense of getting a patent.

"We figured we'd be the only ones that would ever need one," Lamb recalled.

They were wrong. Other froggers began building their own versions of what some called the "Whoosh-mobile."

Today, more than 3,000 airboats whoosh through the Everglades and the marshes and wetlands of Florida. Airboats are used for sightseeing, hunting, fishing, law enforcement, weed control and even warfare. Airboats built in Palm Beach County were used in Vietnam.

But the fact is that frog hunters Lamb and Howard were not the first men to devise the airboat.

Before World War I, Glenn Curtiss, a giant of American aviation, had come to Miami for the winter. A speedster who once held the world's motorcycle speed record of 137 mph,

Scooter, the first airboat, designed to glide through the Everglades, March 5, 1920. (*Photo by Claude Matlack, Historical Association of Southern Florida*)

Curtiss was a designer and inventor of international stature.

Curtiss loved to hunt in the Florida backwoods, usually with bow and arrow. But as frog hunters knew, and Curtiss discovered, getting around in the Everglades was no easy matter.

Curtiss designed, probably on a tablecloth, a shallow-draft motorboat powered by an aircraft engine connected to a propeller mounted on the stern. Unlike the struggling frog hunters, millionaire Curtiss could afford the best of everything.

The boat he designed was enclosed so that a half-dozen people could ride comfortably, protected from the wind. It bore no resemblance to the open-cockpit, scrap iron boat of the frog hunters.

Curtiss called his airboat *Scooter.* It could reach 50 mph slipping over the grassy waters of the Everglades. Later, he designed a smaller airboat capable of 70 mph.

Curtiss engaged one of Miami's most talented photographers, Claude Matlack, to photograph this unusual new boat. One of his photos shows *Scooter* being towed by another boat, apparently in Biscayne Bay. On the back of the picture Matlack had written the date: March 5, 1920.

Since the date of the Lamb/Howard airboat is placed at 1933 by a Florida Game and Fresh Water Fish Commission report, it appears that Curtiss was first with an airboat by at least 13 years. But, like Lamb and Howard, Curtiss failed to patent or market his invention.

Not long after he built the airboat, Curtiss was swept up in the Florida land boom of the 1920s. He developed the cities of Hialeah and Miami Springs, then followed with the bizarre Arabian Nights community of Opa-locka.

Curtiss apparently forgot about the airboat he designed, and it wasn't until Lamb and Howard came up with their design 13 years later that this uniquely Floridian mode of transportation again became a part of the Everglades scene.

PART TWO

The Big Cypress Swamp

Woodsmen of the Big Cypress

The loggers, about 200 of them, set out each Monday morning, riding the train in shacks built on flatcars. Sometimes it took three hours to reach the big trees. The men played penny-ante poker on the 40-mile trip from Copeland into the Big Cypress Swamp.

Non-poker players watched the passing parade of wildlife: deer, otters, bears and panthers. They smiled when the train's wheels sliced up snakes sleeping on the tracks.

This was in the early 1950s, when the Lee Tidewater Cypress Co. was the world's largest cypress logger. Although smaller operators had been logging since the turn of the century, Tidewater owned two-thirds of the cypress timber in Collier County.

Its durability made southern bald cypress one of the most desirable of all woods. The problem was that it grew in the middle of swamps. Northern loggers could rely on rivers to move their wood to the sawmills, but Lee Tidewater had to build a railroad.

To fell the trees, loggers used a technique called girdling. They cut a complete circle into the trees' bark to kill them and drain them of water. Crew members earned about $70 a week. Among the job hazards were roving cottonmouth moccasins.

When work ended on Friday, the men rode the train back to Copeland, a company town built by Tidewater. Their families were waiting, and celebrated with trips to Janes General Store for food, drink and a blaring jukebox.

In its best year, Tidewater moved a third of a billion board feet from Collier County to its mill in Perry, north Florida. When the industry waned in the 1960s, the state began acquiring parcels of the cypress swamp.

Today Copeland is the site of a state prison, and the logging train no longer runs. But its roadbed is still there—used by hikers exploring the 15-mile Fakahatchee Strand trail.

Dragline rig in Big Cypress Swamp, ca. 1950. (*Collier County Historical Museum*)

Saving Corkscrew Swamp

In Collier County the forests of virgin bald cypress stretched for fifty miles, giant trees towering 130 feet above the swampy landscape.

In 1913 the Lee Tidewater Cypress Co. paid $1,400,000 for over 100,000 acres, containing some two-thirds of all the marketable cypress in the county. Nine years later the company gave an option to an agent of Henry Ford, who wanted to buy the Big Cypress Swamp and give it to the State of Florida as a park. The state said it couldn't afford the roads and maintenance the park would involve.

So the lumber companies stepped up their operations, particularly when World War II brought a heavy demand for the durable, rot-resistant wood.

By the early 1950s the only virgin stand of cypress left in southwest Florida stood in the Corkscrew Swamp, near Immokalee. To save what remained, the Corkscrew Cypress Rookery Association was formed in 1954 under the leadership of John H. Baker, president of the National Audubon Society, and O. Earle Frye, Jr., assistant director (later director) of the Florida Game and Fresh Water Fish Commission. Particularly active with the association were Mrs. Eugene A. Smith, of Fort Lauderdale, president of the Florida Federation of Garden Clubs, and Bill Piper, of Everglades Wonder Gardens in Bonita Springs.

The association's goal was "the acquisition and preservation of the greatest remaining bald cypress swamp and its associated plant and animal life." The "associated animal life" included the largest rookery of wood storks and egrets in the country, numbering between 8,000 and 10,000 birds.

Baker moved into action none too soon. Lee Tidewater was preparing to bring its lumber crews into the swamp.

Surprisingly, J. Arthur Currey, president of Lee, proved to be sympathetic to Baker's approach. He agreed to give the group a sizable piece of the company's holdings, grant options on additional acreage and sell the remainder at fair market price.

By December, 1954, $170,000 had been raised to save the Corkscrew Swamp. It came from a variety of sources, among them such industrial magnates as Arthur Vining Davis and John D. Rockefeller, Jr.

Thirty-two hundred additional acres were leased from Collier Enterprises, of Naples, for one dollar a year. Much of this land was later given to the association.

Henry P. "Hank" Bennett, an Audubon warden and wild-life tour leader, was named manager of the Corkscrew Swamp Sanctuary. A one-room cabin with screen porch was built for him by Sam Whidden, a Corkscrew native who had hunted in the area for years.

Sam was soon hired by Bennett to use his construction skills to build a boardwalk into the swamp, a land already

Bob Allen, left, and Warden Hank Bennett study orchids in custard apple pond at Corkscrew Sanctuary, ca. 1955. (*Photo by Allan D. Cruickshank, National Audubon Society*)

Foreman Sam Whidden supervises his brothers, waist deep in water, as they build boardwalk across Corkscrew Sanctuary lettuce pond. (*Photo by Sandy Sprunt, National Audubon Society*)

patrolled by gators, cottonmouth moccasins, leeches, mosquitos, bears and panthers.

The new foreman proved a good recruiter. Bennett himself was promptly put to work on the project, as was Alexander "Sandy" Sprunt IV, who was making an inventory of plants and animals for the National Audubon Society's Research Department, which he now heads. Sam lined up his brothers, Bob and Fletcher, to help with the task of constructing a 5,600-foot walk across a wet, sawgrass prairie, into cypress swamps and even across lakes.

Digging postholes underwater was the toughest part of the job. Said Sprunt: "Poor Hank was rather a short person. I think he stood about five-foot six or seven. He was up to his chin a lot of the time."

Before the boardwalk was built Baker had to lead special guests and potential donors out to the swamp on foot. Once he escorted an influential Miami group that included Dr. Melville Grosvenor, president of the National Geographic Society, Mrs. Grosvenor and Mrs. Carll "Marcia" Tucker, an enthusiastic birder and contributor to the cause. She was at the time in her seventies.

The group walked through sawgrass, swamp and lakes, sometimes in water that was waist-deep. They came out of the swamp dripping wet but glowing with dedication to the cause. After changing into dry clothes, they returned by jeep through cattle ranches until they reached the road where their cars were parked.

The lead car, belonging to Mrs. Tucker, was a shiny, grey Daimler, complete with liveried chauffeur and footman. As the caravan returned to Miami, the Daimler stopped suddenly in front of a raunchy-looking roadside bar. The footman disappeared into the saloon.

One of the directors asked the chauffeur why they had stopped. He was told that Mrs. Tucker had a dry martini, her favorite drink, every afternoon.

Soon the footman reappeared carrying a tray with a martini on it. Mrs. Tucker liked it. She ordered a second one.

By this time villagers and itinerant farm workers had clustered around the Daimler, the first they had ever seen. The martinis might also have been the first they had ever seen.

With two cocktails under her belt, Mrs. Tucker gave the order to resume. The caravan continued to Miami via the Tamiami Trail.

At today's Corkscrew Sanctuary, which is owned and maintained by the National Audubon Society, no martinis are served; in fact, its guidebook states "please no alcoholic beverages." Besides, visitors these days are more interested in observing the country's largest nesting colony of wood storks.

The one question most asked, however, concerns not the birds but the name of the swamp. Actually it backed into its name. A river which rises in the swamp is so crooked in places it was once called the Corkscrew River. The river is now called the Imperial but Corkscrew remains as the name for the swamp and for the sanctuary.

A Missionary

Nobody ever accused Harriet Bedell of standing still. As a missionary in Alaska, the Episcopal deaconess had covered the tractless waste on snowshoes and in dogsleds.

On Florida's Gulf coast, as the missionary to the Seminoles, Bedell moved around the Big Cypress Swamp in a dugout canoe, on horseback and, later, in a second-hand Model-T Ford.

She became a familiar figure in her Model-T, cruising up and down the Tamiami Trail, visiting the Indian camps. She looked after the sick, helped mothers care for their children, and encouraged the Indians to produce better handicrafts— decorated clothing, belts, wood carvings and other salable items.

Bedell, who had no family of her own, came to Florida in 1932 to lecture on Alaska, where she had served the church as a missionary to the Indians for 16 years. She could take the cold; she came from Buffalo.

She didn't like what she saw in Miami. Curious tourists gawked at Indians on display at attractions. "Don't exhibit Indians, exhibit their crafts," she insisted.

Her church's Glade Cross Mission on the western edge of the Everglades had been inactive for 18 years. Time to get it started again, the deaconess decided. Bedell moved the mission site into Everglades City, then the seat of Collier County.

Twenty-seven years with the Indians had taught her patience. She preferred to bring the church's teachings to them on a low-key, one-on-one basis. Seven years elapsed before she brought Indians together for a religious meeting.

Handicrafts provided a way to help the Indians rebuild their self-respect. She believed their arts and crafts were valuable, and proved it by selling them and returning the profits to the artisans.

Deaconess Bedell could be tough on them at times. She rejected any items that were not of the highest quality. She then placed the best of them in South Florida stores. Once a year, in the fall, she loaded up her old car and drove to New York to sell the handicrafts there. She made her solo drive to New York until she was in her 80s.

In 1960, Hurricane Donna swept through Collier County,

Deaconess Harriet Bedell with Seminoles at Indian camp in Big Cypress Swamp, 1940s. (*Fort Lauderdale Historical Society*)

wrecking the Glade Cross Mission. At 85, the deaconess finally
agreed to move to the Bishop Crane Episcopal Home in Dav-
enport, Florida. Even there she didn't really retire, preferring
to continue speaking to groups, preparing Sunday School les-
sons and visiting the sick. Her explanation:

"There is no retirement in the service of the Master."

PART THREE

The Ten Thousand Islands

The Centenarian Hermit of Panther Key

Somehow Old John Gomez made it into the 20th century, quite a feat for a man who said he was born in 1778 in Portugal—or was it the island of Mauritius?

There was usually a fair amount of confusion when Gomez started telling his tall tales. But he was believed to be the oldest man in the United States until he drowned on July 12, 1900, near Panther Key, just south of Marco Island.

A fisherman in his later years, Old John may have caught his foot on the anchor line or the net and been dragged overboard. Or, some suspect, he might have committed suicide. He had become tired of living, explained his 94-year-old wife.

Well, he *had* lived a long time—122 years. And to hear him tell it, it had certainly been a full life.

His eventful career, he said, brought him into contact with world leaders. As a boy he had been patted on the head by Napoleon. As an older man, he claimed to have fought in the Second Seminole War. At the Battle of Lake Okeechobee on December 25, 1837, he served under the command of Zachary Taylor, who would later be elected President of the United States.

What really drew attention to Gomez, though, was his account of his days as a pirate. He sailed, he said, with buccaneer Jose Gaspar, better known as Gasparilla.

Gasparilla is reported to have terrorized the Gulf Coast of Florida in the early 1800s. Legend has it that the bloody reign came to an end in 1822 when he was trapped by an American warship. Rather than face the hangman he wrapped an anchor chain around his waist and drowned himself in the waters near Boca Grande Pass.

With his buccaneer days behind him, John Gomez herded cattle for a while near Cedar Key, then operated as a blockade runner during the Civil War.

John Gomez and his wife on Panther Key, ca. 1890. (*Collier County Historical Museum*)

Finally he settled on one of the Ten Thousand Islands on Florida's southwest coast. He called his island Panther Key because he tried to raise goats there, but the panthers kept eating his stock.

Then, in 1884, at the age of 106, he married a 78-year-old woman he met while on a trip to Tampa, and took her back to his remote island.

For a hermit he attracted a fair number of visitors. People who had heard his Gasparilla tales descended upon Panther Key to dig for treasure. Writers from such national publications as *Forest and Stream* called often to weave stories from his fanciful yarns.

Still, it was never a good idea to underestimate Gomez. Around 1890 a man named Sampson Brown offered to build the centenarian a house from the timbers of a wrecked ship, with the proviso that Old John would will the island to him upon his death. Brown was in his 50s, Gomez over 110. Old John outlived Brown by eight years.

Life Was Cheap
in the Ten Thousand Islands

What remains of the old Watson Place in the Ten Thousand Islands gives little inkling of its bloody, lawless past or the many murders that legend says were committed there. Today, it is just a clearing in the Everglades National Park where boaters on the Wilderness Waterway can camp for the night or break for a picnic.

At the turn of the century, however, the Ten Thousand Islands, a bewildering maze of mangroves, gave cover to fugitives, derelicts and a few harmless hermits. The seven unwritten laws of that wild country, an early account says, were:

1. Suspect every man.
2. Ask no questions.
3. Settle your own quarrels.
4. Never steal from an Islander.
5. Stick by him, even if you do not know him.
6. Shoot quick, when your secret is in danger.
7. Cover your kill.

It was into this last frontier that Ed Watson ventured sometime after 1900. He was a friendly enough man but he was noted, too, for a terrible temper. Rumor had it that he had killed the infamous woman outlaw, Belle Starr, back in the Wild West. True or not, the rumor established Watson as a man to be wary of.

Watson took up farming on the Chatham River, about 10 miles south of Chokoloskee Island on the Gulf Coast. He raised sugar cane, papayas and beans and sold his produce in Key West and Fort Myers.

The newcomer prospered and in time built a dock, a barn and a two-story house. In a land of lean-tos, Watson presented the image of a successful farmer.

Some said he owed his success to cheap labor. In fact, it was suspected he didn't pay his help at all. Most of his workers were fugitives or down-and-outs with no family ties. They worked for Watson, then turned up missing. Many thought they were terminated on payday, but in keeping with the code of the region, nobody asked any questions.

Then, after a brawl in Fort Myers, three men went to

The Ed Watson place in the Ten Thousand Islands. (*Historical Association of Southern Florida*)

Chatham Bend to "get" Watson. A shootout followed. Nobody was killed but one of the men had half of his mustache shot off. People began to call Watson the "Barber"—but not to his face.

Living with Watson at Chatham Bend in the fall of 1910 were five people, among them a large woman named Hannah Smith who was known as Big Six, a man named Leslie Cox and an old black man whose name was not known. In October of that year, a group of Chokoloskee clam-diggers discovered the body of Big Six near Watson's place.

Soon afterwards, the old black man turned up in Chokoloskee with confused tales of murders at Chatham Bend. Watson arrived next. He admitted there had been murders but said that Cox had committed them.

The people on Chokoloskee wanted the sheriff to investigate. But the sheriff didn't want to go to Chatham Bend. A hurricane in October, 1910, may have altered the sheriff's plans. It certainly affected Watson's future. Watson set off to hunt for Cox with storm-wet shotgun shells.

Later that month, Watson arrived again in Chokoloskee, carrying a shotgun in one hand and a pistol on his hip. Unfortunately for him, most of the crowd that greeted him also carried guns.

Watson told the crowd that he had killed Cox, and for proof produced a hat he said belonged to Cox. The crowd was unconvinced, although some of the men agreed to return to Chatham Bend to see the body. Someone raised the question of whether Watson should be allowed to carry his gun. An argument followed and Watson pulled both the shotgun's triggers. The gun, loaded with wet shells, misfired. At that point, practically the whole crowd blazed away at Watson. So many bullets pierced his body that no one knew who really killed him. And no one tried very hard to find out.

Whether Watson had really killed Cox, or which if either of them killed Big Six, remains a mystery to this day. Cox, for his part, was never heard from again.

On Chokoloskee, Each Man Was an Island

Chokoloskee Island, stepping-off point to the Ten Thousand Islands, is less than 150 acres in size—yet it has seen more than its share of rugged individualists over the years.

Probably the first white settler in the area was Captain Dick Turner, sometime in the 1870s. He had been a scout for the U.S. Army during the Third Seminole War, in the 1850s, and gave his name to the scenic Turner River, a stream highly regarded by today's canoeists.

C. G. McKinney, the man who would become the "Sage of Chokoloskee," came to the island in 1886. He started the island's first store and its first post office, and was widely known for years as a newspaper correspondent, given to a picturesque turn of phrase. Under his pen, mosquitos became "swamp angels" and moonshine whiskey "low bush lightning."

McKinney's business policy was spelled out on his store's letterhead: "No Banking. No Mortgaging. No Insurance. No Borrowing. No Loaning. I must have cash to buy more hash."

For people who think today's schools are overwhelmed by problems, here's what McKinney wrote about the Chokoloskee School in 1924: "Our schoolteacher . . . is going to give up her school today, it is too much for her nerves. She seems to be a nice refined body and we are sorry for her. She had a trying time here, but we can give her praise for her endurance. Maybe we don't need any school—we all know enough anyway. They seem to learn to chew tobacco, curse and drink booze at an early age and think their education is complete when they have these necessities ground into their topknots."

The best known of all latter-day Chokoloskee figures was Ted Smallwood. He came to the island in the 1890s and operated the settlement's biggest store as well as its post office.

Because Chokoloskee Bay was so shallow, only the smallest of boats could make it in to his trading post. Without waiting for the Corps of Engineers, Ted just dredged a channel several hundred yards long from his dock out to deep water.

A 1924 hurricane blew in Ted Smallwood's front door, moved four feet of water into his store and lifted it off its foundation. This was warning enough for Ted. He built pilings and

Ted Smallwood in doorway of his store, ca. 1930. (*Historical Association of Southern Florida*)

raised his store eight feet, just in time to protect the property from the devastating September, 1926 hurricane.

A colorful man with a bushy, handlebar mustache, Smallwood lived until 1943. His daughter Thelma ran the store until her death four decades later. The old building still stands, but it is no longer operating as a store.

"In Thelma's will she left it to the park (Everglades National Park) or if we couldn't work it out, to the state," said her brother Glen Smallwood, in his seventies and still an active charter boat captain. "Pretty soon, we'll have it worked out."

Captain Smallwood is confident that the old store his father built in 1917 will be preserved—a monument to the pioneering spirit of the Ten Thousand Islands.

Clam Diggers of Marco Island

Not so long ago, Florida was short on ways to make a living. You could farm, hunt and fish. And if you lived on Marco Island you had one added opportunity—clams.

It was hard work, particularly around the turn of the century. But in its heyday, the clam industry provided jobs for some 200 people on the island.

Clam diggers stalked their quarry in knee-deep water, feeling for the mollusks with their bare feet and hoping they didn't happen to step on a stingray. Boats from the canneries cruised by and bought the catch at 25 cents a bushel. On a good day a digger might harvest 30 bushels worth $7.50.

Along Florida's southwest coast lay some of the largest clam beds in the United States, covering about 150 miles of sea bottom. One, below Marco, was said to be 20 miles long and loaded with clams as large as a man's two fists.

However, Captain Bill Collier, the biggest landowner on the island, had concluded that digging clams by hand wasn't

Clamboat on its way to cannery on Marco Island. (*Collier County Historical Museum*)

efficient because the digging had to be limited to shallow water, low tides and calm seas.

In 1908, Collier invented a clam-dredging machine that worked so well it put most of the individual diggers out of business. The dredge brought up clams from as deep as 12 feet. With a crew of 25, it could gather 500 bushels of clams in a 12-hour shift.

With the dramatic increase in clams came the need for a new cannery. Collier brought J. H. Doxsee, whose family had been canning clams in Islip, Long Island, since 1867, to Marco to set up a cannery.

The Doxsees operated from 1910 to 1947. When the clam beds became "fished out" and the cannery closed, Marco plunged into deep depression until the 1960s. Then the island was parceled into plush real estate developments which promised their buyers "island living." But it was hardly the kind of island living those early clam diggers knew.

PART FOUR

The Florida Keys

Jose Marti in Key West

In appearance he was not an impressive man. He was pale, thin and tense. His mustache drooped and his hairline receded.

But when Jose Marti spoke, crowded factories and convention halls fell silent. His oratory, some said, could "wring tears from a corpse."

Born in Havana in 1853, Marti grew up on an island which lived under Spanish rule. He was a rebellious youth. When he was only 16, his legs were manacled with chains for advocating Cuban independence.

Deported to Spain, Marti earned three university diplomas and began to realize that he was blessed with a gift for public speaking.

He learned English, convinced that his base of operations would have to be the United States. That was where Cuban exiles were keeping alive the dream of a free homeland.

In 1891 he came to the U.S., visiting New York and the two Florida cities where the exiles were concentrated—Tampa and Key West, then the state's most populous city. His greatest support came from the cigar makers. Many of them gave him 10 percent of their earnings.

By 1892 Marti had organized a chain of local organizations into the new Cuban Revolutionary Party. Key West alone had 61 freedom clubs, Tampa 16. At that time there was no Miami.

In Key West he would speak at the home of Teodoro Perez at Duval and Catherine Streets. Perez owned a cigar factory and served as secretary of the Cigar Manufacturers Union.

(The house where Marti visited still bears his name. Now a pink-hued guest house and restaurant, it is called La Terraza de Marti, better known as La Te Da.)

At a gathering of Cuban exiles in Tampa, Marti declared,

Jose Marti, second from right, behind child, in Key West, 1892. (*Historical Association of Southern Florida*)

"I should want the cornerstone of our Republic to be the devotion of Cubans to the full dignity of man. Either the Republic has as its foundation ... the unrestricted freedom of others—in short, the passion for man's essential worth—or else the Republic is not worth a single one of the tears of our women nor a solitary drop of a brave man's blood."

In 1895 it was the blood of Marti himself that was shed. Returning to Cuba to join the troops fighting Spain, he was killed one moonlit evening in a surprise attack by the Spaniards.

Jose Marti lived only 42 years, not long enough to see Cuba win her independence from Spain. Nearly a century after his death, Cuba's greatest national hero lends his name to still another effort to gain freedom for Cuba. It is the U.S.-funded, anti-Communist broadcasting station called Radio Marti.

The Spanish-American War and Key West

Secretary of State John Hay called it "a splendid little war." Some would argue that his description of the Spanish-American War was not quite accurate.

In Key West, a better word would have been "thirsty," but decidedly not "splendid."

Key West, 90 miles from Cuba, was an important strategic location. With a large Cuban population, the city was a hotbed of agitation for independence for Cuba. Fanned by inflammatory political rhetoric and sensational "yellow" journalism, the cause of a free Cuba erupted into a war between a young lion of a nation, spoiling for a fight, and a tired old tiger, preferring to be left alone.

On January 24, 1898, the *USS Maine* left Key West bound for Havana Harbor, ostensibly on a friendly visit—but actually sent to flex U.S. muscles. Three weeks later, the *Maine* blew up in the harbor, killing 268 Americans. To this day no one knows what caused the explosion—but Americans blamed Spain, remembered the *Maine* and declared war.

U.S. troops embarking for Cuba during the Spanish-American War, 1898. (*Florida Photographic Archives*)

Army and Navy servicemen and supplies poured into the tiny island of Key West. The town's three-man police force reeled from the rapid arrival of 10,000 soldiers. Street brawls erupted, as well as racial conflicts between black soldiers and white residents.

The biggest problem was thirst. The winter had been a dry one, leaving the island's cisterns low at just the time when an army of drinkers showed up. Barges loaded with 100,000 gallons of water were towed to Key West from as far away as St. Petersburg.

The real solution turned out to be plants to distill fresh water from the salt water that surrounded the island. The Navy cranked up an old distillery it had built during the Civil War. Soldiers hurriedly built new plants. By early June the problem was solved. And, naturally, that's when the rains came.

Key West Spongers Built an Empire

Look in my trunk and see what's there, sponger money,
One hundred dollars was my share, sponger money,
Sponger money never done, sponger money . . .

Old Conch folk song

Not so long ago, Key West was the sponging capitol of the world. In 1895, some 1400 men and 300 boats were busy harvesting sponges from the floor of the shallow seas off the island city. It all added up to sponger money, money that was badly needed in a town that had seen two of its major sources of income—wreck salvaging and cigar-making—come and go.

Like the wreckers and the cigar-makers before them, Key West's spongers would enjoy only a brief moment of glory. But while it lasted, sponger money meant a hot time in town when the sponging boats came back to the docks at the foot of Elizabeth Street.

The sponge market started in 1849, when a New York freighter picked up a load of Key West sponges, at that time generally thought to be of little value. When the captain found a ready market for them, he returned and told the Conchs he would take all the quality sponges they could gather.

A sponge explosion followed. Within a few years, Key West was supplying 90 percent of all the sponges bought by Americans for industrial, hospital and home use.

The Conch approach to sponge-harvesting was primitive but effective. Two men worked from a small boat, one rowing, the other spotting the sponges through a glass-bottomed bucket and then gathering them with a long three-pronged pole. Bigger operations involved a schooner, towing eight to ten dinghies. The schooner might stay out as long as three months—however long it took to fill the boats with sponges.

Key West knew when the sponging boats were coming back. The smell of sponges drying ran miles ahead of them. No one liked the smell, but everyone liked sponger money.

In 1904, Greek colonists broke Key West's sponge monopoly by introducing hard-hat sponge diving from a base in Tar-

Sponges and spongers on Key West docks, ca. 1900. (*Historical Association of Southern Florida*)

pon Springs. The Conchs did not give up without a fight. They burned two of the invading Greeks' boats, slashed air hoses and smashed equipment. But theirs was a losing battle. Wasteful methods of sponge harvesting over the years had depleted the Keys' beds, and the Conchs' primitive approach to sponging did not permit them to compete with the hard-hat divers farther afield.

Today, in Tarpon Springs, synthetic substitutes have turned the former Sponge Exchange into a shopping mall. And, in Key West, a handful of spongers still gather a small harvest, sold locally to the tourists. "Sponger money never done" is a phrase that now simply echoes a part of the Conch capitol's colorful past.

Working on the Overseas Railroad

Nobody ever said building a railroad from Homestead to Key West would be easy. It would have to reach more than a hundred miles into the Atlantic, connect scores of tiny islands, bridge deep, swift-flowing channels, and withstand the force of hurricanes.

Henry M. Flagler, owner of the Florida East Coast Railway, called it the toughest job he ever undertook. For the men who did the brutal manual labor, it was even tougher.

Construction began in 1905. The men had to battle heat, sand flies, rattlesnakes, alligators, crocodiles, and worst of all, mosquitos. In October 1906, a hurricane claimed the lives of at least 130 men. By the time the job was finished, the death toll was enormous.

Construction camps were built all along the Keys. Camp 10 was on Key Vaca, which became the project's headquarters. "Building this railroad has become a regular marathon," one worker remarked. Henceforth Camp 10 was known as Marathon—today the second-largest city in the Keys.

Payday for railroad workers in Florida Keys, 1906. (*Florida Photographic Archives*)

Flagler drew his work force from as far away as Spain and Italy, many laborers were blacks from the Caribbean. But the bulk came from good, solid American stock: to wit, winos from the skid rows of New York and Philadelphia. The pay: $1.25 a day.

One of the biggest problems was keeping the winos sober. Flagler banned liquor in the work camps but enterprising Key Westers maneuvered around the ban with "Booze Boats." Strait-laced residents countered with "Preacher Boats," sent to hold religious services.

Finally, after seven years, the 156-mile railroad reached Key West, on January 22, 1912. It had taken the labor of 20,000 men, and cost $50 million—more than half a billion in present-day dollars.

Remembering the Big Pine Inn

Wayfarers heading to Key West on U.S. 1 used to see an imposing, two-story wooden building to their left as they cruised across Big Pine Key. It was called Big Pine Inn.

You could stop for the night; the inn had 12 rooms, renting for eight dollars a night as recently as the 1960s. Or you could have a drink or a meal. The turtle steak was superb.

That all changed in the early morning hours of December 17, 1978. After more than 70 years, the inn's Dade County pine had simply dried out. Fire broke out and the Lower Keys lost a memorable landmark.

Mrs. Gussie Zeigner started construction of the inn in 1906, before Henry Flagler's railroad reached the area. The building materials—pine and cypress—had to be shipped in

Big Pine Inn on Big Pine Key, late 1920's. (*Monroe County Public Library*)

by boat. Once the crew went on strike and Gussie unloaded the boards herself.

After completion, the inn welcomed many of the railroad's executives, including Flagler. At one time, the railroad's ticket window was located in the inn. Later it would also house the local post office.

It became a gathering place of note, comfortable even in the hot Keys summers thanks to its high ceiling fans. Author James McLendon wrote: "During the'20s and '30s many a good time was had at the inn. Here bonded bootleg whiskey, good meals and gambling would relieve you of your money in every socially accepted way."

The inn's popularity increased further when Flagler's roadbed became the foundation for U.S. 1 after the 1935 hurricane demolished the tracks. From the inn's windows guests could see tiny Key deer, an endangered species found principally in Big Pine.

Then came the fire. Where the famous Big Pine Inn once stood, a bank building has now arisen.

Going Batty on Sugarloaf Key

All anyone remembers about Richter Clyde Perky is a little settlement in the Florida Keys called Perky—and a bat tower.

It's an unusual legacy for a man whose dream of a boom-time resort was swept away in cloud after cloud of fierce salt-marsh mosquitos.

A Coloradan, Perky bought nearly all of Sugarloaf Key in 1919 for $10,000 and brought his considerable land development and sales skills to bear on the island venture. But he didn't count on blood-thirsty mosquitos attacking visitors, making Sugarloaf Key virtually uninhabitable.

Perky reacted with a bold move. He had heard of the work of Dr. Charles Campbell, a San Antonio physician, who had sought to hold down the population of malarial mosquitos by bringing bats in to eat them. His ideas were presented in many scholarly journals and in a 1925 book, *Bats, Mosquitos and Dollars*.

Dr. Campbell had designed and patented a special bat tower to serve as a home for friendly, mosquito-munching bats. Perky should have been more wary. One of the good doctor's seven towers was erected on the grounds of an insane asylum, perhaps a check on the bats-in-the-belfry syndrome.

In between swats, Perky bought plants and bat bait from the Texan. He built two 30-foot, cedar-shingled towers of Dade County pine. Above the flat Lower Keys landscape the towers loomed like windmills without blades.

Campbell also sold Perky a magical potion of bat bait, a loathsome concoction of bat droppings and ground-up sex organs of female bats. It was shipped in a small pine box resembling a coffin.

Placed on the earthen floors of the towers, the bat bait was allowed to go to work. Nose-witness accounts describe the smell as so sickening that people working nearby had to keep their distance. So did the bats.

There is no evidence that any bat ever roomed at the towers. And yet, the towers and the bat bait cost Perky more than he paid for the island itself.

Legend has it that Keys mosquitos ate the bats, not the other way around. At any rate, the mosquito problem was never solved until massive spraying of the Keys years later.

Today one of Perky's towers still stands, designated a historic landmark. An inscription on its base reads: "Dedicated to good health at Perky, Fla., by Mr. and Mrs. R. C. Perky, March 15, 1929."

The Bat Tower on Sugarloaf Key. (*Florida Photographic Archives*)

Craig Key, Population: One

On Craig Key nothing was quite as it seemed. Poor Old Craig wasn't exactly poor, and Poor Old Craig's Hotel wasn't exactly operated as a home for the indigent.

Furthermore, Craig wasn't exactly a key; it was just a good-sized landfill, dating back to Florida Keys railroad construction in the early 1900s. And Craig wasn't really a town. It had just one full-time resident—Roland Craig.

But Craig had a post office. It was granted to the one-man town, the story goes, to make it easier for an important national figure to pick up his mail when cruising through the Keys. The visitor was an enthusiastic fisherman named Herbert Hoover, president from 1929 to 1933.

Roland Craig, who came to Florida from Ohio, was particularly proud of President Hoover's patronage. His fishing lodge, located just above Long Key, catered to a few wealthy sportsmen who felt the unimpressive look of Poor Old Craig's Hotel guaranteed an obscure hideaway.

Inside, the lodge was a good deal less stark. Its six rooms were attractively decorated. Food was good, including what was claimed to be "the best key lime pie in the Keys."

Craig's fiefdom also included Craig's Store, which sold groceries, beer, fishing tackle and water, five cents a gallon; Craig's Bar, offering beer, wine, whiskey, poker, craps and slot machines, around the clock; Craig's Service Station; and Craig's Marina.

Craig also invested with considerable success in Keys land. He used to show up at Miami casinos, his pockets bulging with cash, cheerfully announcing, "Here comes Poor Old Craig."

Hurricane Donna in 1960 destroyed five of the seven buildings on Craig Key. The Florida State Road Department, which leased the land to Craig, ordered the other two demolished, then reclaimed the fill.

When Craig went back to Miami, Keys pioneer Del Layton had the post office moved to his nearby town, Layton, on Long Key. At first the federal government made him use the name "Craig Post Office" and the road department compounded the insult by erecting "Craig" signs on either end of the mile-long village of Layton.

Poor Old Craig's Hotel in Florida Keys. (*Monroe County Public Library*)

"Funny thing about those road signs," recalled Layton. "They kept disappearing." So did the identity of Craig, who died years ago.

In time the U.S. government renamed its postal outlet "Long Key Post Office" and Del's town became Layton, not Craig.

Poor Old Craig.

Big Hunt for a Little Key Deer

They called him "el aeroplano," a tiny Key deer so fast he seemed to fly. El aeroplano eluded hunters for 10 years before he was finally bagged on Big Torch Key, with the aid of a legendary deerhound named "Ha-Ha."

That was in the 1930s, when deer hunting flourished in the Keys. Most of the deer hunters were Cubans, former cigarmakers from Key West, who used "exploradores," the Spanish equivalent of hunting guides. It was one of the exploradores, a man named Tertulino, who bagged el aeroplano.

Tertulino and Julio Pui were considered the island city's two most effective exploradores, each man serving his particular group of followers as "el capitan" of the hunt.

"I have hunted deer on the Keys for many, many years," Pui told author Stetson Kennedy, "and my father he hunt before me. Also, I have hunt deer in Cuba and the West Indies."

The Key deer is a subspecies, a smaller version of the North American white-tail, less than three feet high at the shoulder. A buck averages 65 to 80 pounds, a doe about 40. Over many years the deer has adapted to the aquatic world of the Keys.

"They are very clean, have few ticks, and their flesh is of excellent flavor," said Pui. "And fast—they almost fly."

By the 1930s, hunting had depleted the number of Key deer to 20. In 1939 the Florida Legislature banned deer hunting in the Keys. Since then, the efforts of many conservationists and agencies have helped the tiny deer to make a comeback. The effort culminated in 1963 with the dedication of the National Key Deer Refuge.

Today, between 250 and 300 tiny deer roam the Florida Keys, mostly on Big Pine and No-Name Keys and protected within the roughly 7,000 acres managed by the National Key Deer Refuge.

Under the care of the U.S. Fish and Wildlife Service, the population once rose to a high of 400. But new dangers have again reduced their numbers. Development is shrinking their habitat, dogs are harassing them, and cars have taken their toll. More than 60 were killed by motorists in 1987.

But the Key deer survive, just as in the days of el aeroplano. And today, stalkers are more likely to be armed with

Key deer hunter with hounds and trophies in Lower Keys, late 1930s. (*Stetson Kennedy*)

curiosity and a camera than a gun. Says Charlie Case, assistant refuge manager: "The best way to see the deer is to drive out to Key Deer Boulevard on Big Pine late in the evening. That's when you'll see them."

Harry Truman, the Conch President

Some would say Harry S. Truman made Key West richer just by drawing world attention to the island city during his 11 working vacations there as president. More tourists, more dollars.

On March 12, 1949, Truman directly made a lot of Key West numbers players richer—and a few "bolita" houses a good deal poorer.

In the arcane world of numbers wagering (known in Spanish as bolita), "45" stands for president. And since Truman was greeted with the traditional 21-gun salute, numbers players all over the island bought the 21–45 combination. It hit, at odds of 80 to 1.

No wonder they loved him in Key West. One of the city's main streets, Truman Avenue, is named after him. His daughter is remembered through the Margaret Truman Launderette.

Harry Truman made Key West the Little White House in the late fall of 1946, partly because the submarine base there had ample accommodations, already located on secure government property, and partly because he needed warmer weather to shake a lingering cold. On November 18 he wrote his mother:

"I left Washington yesterday morning in a rain and a fog with a temperature at 40 degrees. Arrived here at three p.m. in sunshine and 80 degrees. They put me up in a Southern-built house with galleries all around, upstairs and down . . . I've just returned from the beach . . . and my cough and cold are nearly gone already."

During another visit in 1948, on November 11, he wrote his sister, pointing out that Armistice Day was particularly special for him, dating back to his service in World War I:

"I am on my way to the beach to take a swim. Just 30 years ago I was firing a final barrage at the heinies at a little town . . . northeast of Verdun. Some change of position, I'd say."

The relaxing spell of Key West engulfed the president. Once he unexpectedly called a press conference. Reporters anticipating an earth-shaking announcement saw the president walk in wearing a loud tropical shirt and a pith helmet.

It turned out to be a reverse press conference, with Tru-

President Truman in Key West, late 1940s. (*Monroe County Public Library*)

man asking all the questions: How late were they out last night? Had they had breakfast? Had they written their wives in the past week?

One of the biggest laughs for Harry Truman, wife Bess and daughter Margaret came when a 1950 census taker showed up at the Little White House. She asked the president what his occupation was.